20 FUN FACTS ABOUT

BATS

By Heather Moore Niver

Gareth Stevens
Publishing

Please visit our website, www.garethstevens.com. For a free color catalog of all our high-quality books, call toll free 1-800-542-2595 or fax 1-877-542-2596.

For Robyn and Zoe

Library of Congress Cataloging-in-Publication Data

Niver, Heather Moore.
20 fun facts about bats / Heather Moore Niver.
    p. cm. — (Fun fact file: Animals!)
Includes index.
ISBN 978-1-4339-6507-4 (pbk.)
ISBN 978-1-4339-6508-1 (6-pack)
ISBN 978-1-4339-6505-0 (library binding)
1. Bats—Miscellanea—Juvenile literature. I. Title. II. Title: Twenty fun facts about bats.
QL737.C5N58 2012
599.4—dc23

               2011021357

First Edition

Published in 2012 by
Gareth Stevens Publishing
111 East 14th Street, Suite 349
New York, NY 10003

Copyright © 2012 Gareth Stevens Publishing

Designer: Michael J. Flynn
Editor: Greg Roza

Photo credits: Cover, pp. 1, 5, 6–7, 8, 9, 11, 12, 13, 15, 18, 19, 20, 21, 22, 23, 25, 27, 29 Shutterstockcom; p. 14 Nick Gordon/Oxford Scientific/Getty Images; p. 16 Carol Farneti Foster/Oxford Scientific/Getty Images; p. 17 Otis Imboden/National Geographic/Getty Images; p. 24 Michael Durham/Minden Pictures/Getty Images; p. 26 Bloomberg/Getty Images.

Printed in the United States of America

CPSIA compliance information: Batch #CW12GS: For further information contact Gareth Stevens, New York, New York at 1-800-542-2595.

Contents

Words in the glossary appear in **bold** type the first time they are used in the text.

Behold the Bat!

Bats may be one of the most misunderstood animals around. Many of us have heard strange stories about bats turning into vampires or getting stuck in people's hair. Bats are actually shy and tend to avoid people.

Bats are often mistaken for other animals, such as mice or birds. Actually, they're flying **mammals**. They're clean, fuzzy animals that spend lots of time keeping their fur soft. Their fur can be shades of brown, tan, gray, or black, with bits of red, yellow, or orange.

Black flying fox bats live mainly along the northern coast of Australia.

So, What Is a Bat?

FACT 1

Bats aren't furry birds or flying mice.

Because they fly, bats are sometimes confused with birds. Some people call bats "flying mice." But bats aren't like birds or mice at all. Scientists put bats in their own group called Chiroptera (ky-RAHP-tuh-ruh), which means "hand-wing."

Up, Up, and Away!

FACT 2

Bats can be as big as an eagle or as small as a bee.

Giant bats called flying foxes have a **wingspan** of up to 6.6 feet (2 m). Bumblebee bats are the smallest mammals in the world. They weigh less than a dime and have a wingspan of about 6 inches (15 cm).

giant flying fox bat

Bat fingers have the same number of bones that ours do. However, they're longer and skinnier.

FACT 3

Bats have fingers and thumbs—just like you.

Thumbs help bats walk, climb, and hold food. A bat's thumb is small, but it has a claw. It looks like bats don't have fingers, but check out their wings! They have four long, skinny fingers on each "hand," or wing.

Bats and frogs have something in common.

Bats have thin, rubbery skin between their fingers just like frogs have skin between their toes. Bats use this skin to fly just like frogs use it to swim. Some bats fly up to 20 miles (32 km) an hour!

Making Sense of Bat Senses

FACT 5

If you're "blind as a bat," you can see pretty well.

Most bats see as well as humans. Bat eyes work well in the dark. Most bats see in black and white. However, fruit bats see some color. Fruit bats can have large eyes that gather lots of light. Insect-eating bats usually have smaller eyes.

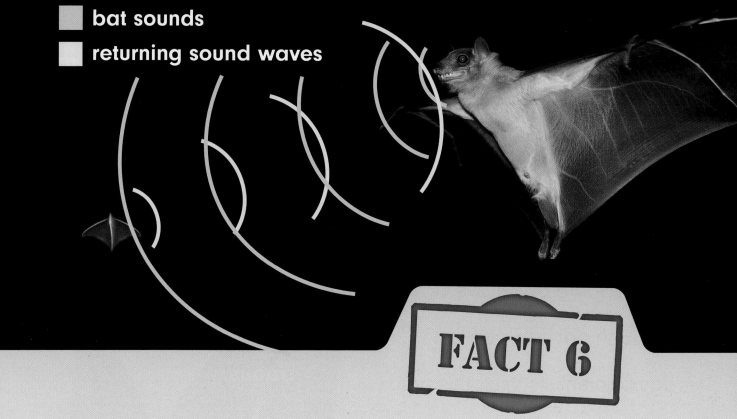

bat sounds
returning sound waves

Bats can "see" in total darkness by using sound.

Some bats use a process called **echolocation** to locate hard-to-see objects. Bats "shout" loudly and figure out how far away something is by how long it takes for the sound to bounce back from the object. People can't usually hear these sounds.

Bats with bigger ears hear more sounds.

Bats' ears collect lots of sounds. The bigger their ears, the more they can hear. This means their echolocation calls can be quieter. Some bats have a flap of skin on each ear called a tragus. Scientists think this helps them hear, too.

tragus

Leaf-nosed bats have a flap of skin above their noses. Scientists think the flap may aid them in echolocation.

FACT 8

A mother bat can find her baby in the dark by smell alone.

Bats have an excellent sense of smell. Fruit bats use it to find food. Bats mark themselves and other bats in their colony with a certain smell. This may be how they find their colonies.

What's on the Bat Menu?

Vampire bats are the only mammals that eat nothing but blood.

Yes, vampire bats drink blood. Most get it from livestock or birds—not people! They only need a small helping of blood every night. There are more than 1,100 kinds of bats, but only three kinds are vampire bats.

This vampire bat is feeding on blood from a horse.

WHAT'S FOR DINNER?

Just
3 kinds of
bats eat blood.

A few bats eat frogs,
mice, birds, fish, or other bats.

Some bats eat **nectar** from flowers.

Many bats eat fruit.

Seventy percent of the bats in the
world eat insects.

This bat has caught a frog for dinner!

FACT 10

A mother bat can eat her own weight in insects each night.

Many bats eat insects. If you don't like mosquitoes, you might be happy to know that the little brown bat can eat up to 1,000 mosquitoes an hour! Some bats eat frogs, birds, and even other kinds of bats!

FACT 11

Some bats have tongues longer than their body.

Some bats use their long tongues to get nectar from flowers. Desert bats drink nectar from cactus flowers. Nectar bats use their long tongues to get their food. The tube-lipped nectar bat is the size of a small mouse, but its tongue is about 3.5 inches (8.9 cm) long!

Bats and Flowers

Bats help flowers and trees grow.

As fruit bats fly, they drop seeds from fruit they've eaten. This helps grow new trees. Nectar bats **pollinate** flowers. As they drink, pollen gets on their face. It rubs off at the next flower. The pollen helps the plant make fruit.

COMMON FOODS POLLINATED BY BATS

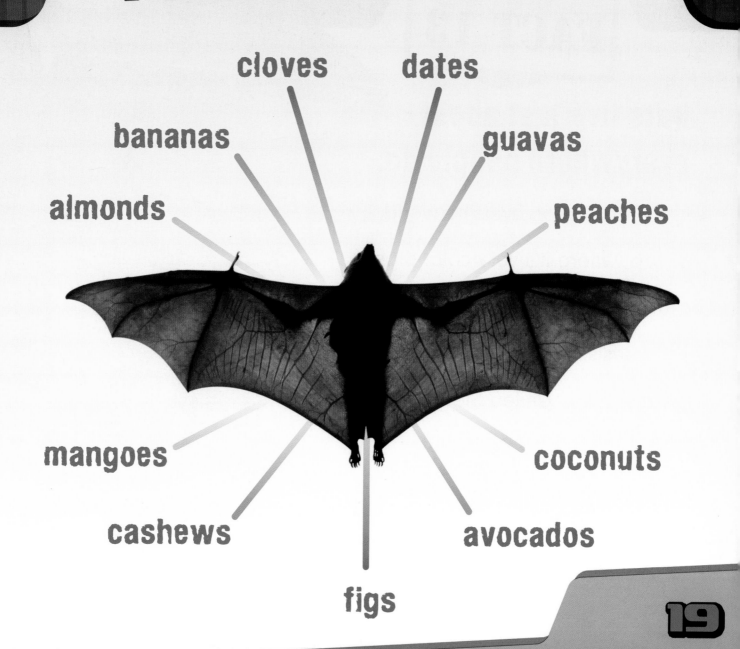

cloves

dates

bananas

guavas

almonds

peaches

mangoes

coconuts

cashews

avocados

figs

At Home with Bats

FACT 13

Bats live just about everywhere people do.

Bats live all over the world, except where it's very cold. Most of the world's bats prefer jungles or rainforests. There are about 45 kinds of bats in the United States. Most live in the warmer southern states.

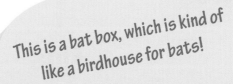

This is a bat box, which is kind of like a birdhouse for bats!

This is a colony of red flying fox bats roosting in a tree.

Bats spend all day sleeping upside down.

Bats sleep, or roost, all day while hanging from their feet!

Their toes and claws are curved so they don't fall. Many bats

like to roost in hidden places, such as in caves or under tree

bark. Others sleep out in the open.

Hibernating bats often sleep close together to keep warm.

FACT 15

Some bats go all winter without eating.

Some bats rest or sleep all winter while the weather is cold and food is hard to find. This is called hibernation. The bats eat lots of food in the summer and fall to keep them from going hungry while they're hibernating.

On the "Road" with Bats

Some bats travel to warmer areas for the winter.

Some bats fly to warmer parts of the world for the winter. This is called migration. Food is easier to find in warmer places. Sometimes the bats fly back and forth between the same roosts year after year.

Batty Families

FACT 17

More than 20 million bats live in Bracken Cave in Texas each summer.

Many bats live in colonies. The colonies may be huge. However, each bat family is small. A bat mother usually has only one baby, or pup, each year. Bats live about 20 years. One bat is said to have lived for 41 years!

Bracken Cave

Vampire bats have been known to raise young bats that have lost their parents.

FACT 18

Bat babies learn how to fly by the time they're 3 weeks old.

Baby bats are blind and deaf at birth. Strong back legs help them hang on to their mothers in the roost. A mother bat feeds her pup milk from her body. The pups grow quickly and are flying within 3 weeks.

Staying Alive!

Bats have existed for about 50 million years.

Bats have been around much longer than people, but some are in danger of dying out. Several kinds of US bats are **endangered**. In the wild, bats are hunted by animals such as owls and snakes. An illness called white-nose **syndrome** is killing many bats. Other bats die when people destroy the forests and caves where they live.

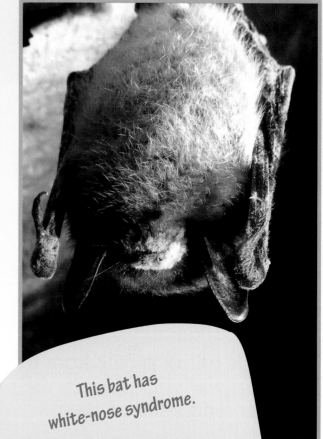

This bat has white-nose syndrome.

Wind turbines, like the ones shown here, help create clean energy. However, they can harm bats that fly into them.

A bat may have saved your favorite food.

Bats help with more than pollination. Bat **guano** has been used as a **fertilizer** for many years. Bats that hunt insects help control pests that ruin crops. Mexican free-tailed bats love to dine on corn earworm moths, which destroy crops such as watermelon.

Batty About Bats!

Once you get past some of the silly stories and learn the facts, you realize that bats are helpful, interesting animals. For example, echolocation works better than anything humans have invented for flying around the dark night skies.

Bats have been around for 50 million years. That means they've been around much longer than humans! They're important for pollination and pest control. People need to help keep bat homes safe. That way, bats can hang around for another 50 million years!

You can see this vampire bat's pointy teeth, which allow the bat to break an animal's skin and get to its blood.

29

Glossary

echolocation: a way of locating objects by producing sounds that bounce off objects

endangered: in danger of dying out

fertilizer: something that makes soil better for growing crops and other plants

guano: bat or bird droppings

mammal: a warm-blooded animal that has a backbone and hair, breathes air, and feeds milk to its young

nectar: a sweet liquid found in flowers

pollinate: to take pollen from one flower, plant, or tree to another

syndrome: an illness or disorder

wingspan: the length between the tips of a pair of wings that are stretched out

For More Information

Books

Carney, Elizabeth. *Bats.* Washington, DC: National Geographic, 2010.

Iorio, Nicole, and Time for Kids Staff. *Bats!* New York, NY: HarperCollins Publishers, 2005.

Websites

All About Bats: Kidz Cave
www.batcon.org/index.php/all-about-bats/kidz-cave.html
The Kidz Cave includes lots of fun bat games, quizzes, and activities to help you learn more about bats.

Bat World: Kids Page
www.batworld.org/kids-page/
Watch bat videos, do puzzles, and find out how fun bats can be.

Lubee Bat Conservancy
www.batconservancy.org/kids-and-teacher-bat-resources
At the Lubee Bat Conservancy website, you can learn more about bats with a comic book and games.

Index